B
Br

Dr Clemency Mitchell

First published in 2010
Copyright © 2010 Autumn House Publishing
(Europe) Ltd.
All rights reserved. No part of this publication
may be reproduced in any form without prior
permission from the publisher.
British Library Cataloguing in Publication
Data. A catalogue record for this book is
available from the British Library.
ISBN 978-1-906381-81-3
Published by Autumn House, Grantham,
Lincolnshire, England.
Designed by Lydia Hamblin
Printed in Thailand.

Breakfast is VERY IMPORTANT.

According to Mrs Beeton, the great English cookery writer, the moral and physical wellbeing of mankind depends largely upon its breakfast.

Eating breakfast is one of the seven health habits most closely associated with longevity, as important as regular exercise and not smoking.

Better breakfasts

Workers who eat breakfast are more efficient; schoolchildren who eat breakfast are calmer and get better grades.

Thousands of researchers have confirmed these and many other benefits of a nourishing breakfast, including better concentration at school and work, better temper, better behaviour, better control of blood sugar, weight and cholesterol, stronger immune system and better control of addictions.

For optimum performance, our bodies, like cars at the start of a trip, need a good supply of appropriate fuel to begin the day.

Better breakfasts

To get the best from our food it needs to look good and taste good, we need the right amount at the right time, and it does us most good if we eat it in a cheerful frame of mind.

This book brings a variety of suggestions to keep breakfast interesting, whether you want your breakfast quick and cheerful for every day or leisurely and luxurious for holidays.

'Grains, fruits, nuts, and vegetables constitute the diet chosen for us by our Creator. These foods, prepared in as simple and natural a manner as possible, are the most healthful and nourishing. They impart a strength, a power of endurance, and a vigour of intellect, that are not afforded by a more complex and stimulating diet.'
Ellen G. White, *Counsels on Diet and Foods,* p. 363.

This is a VEGETARIAN cookbook.

More than that, it is a STRICT VEGETARIAN cookbook. Only plant foods are used, and usually whole plant foods at that.

That simply means grains, fruits, nuts, seeds and vegetables prepared in simple, natural ways. The healing properties of plant foods are the reason for the longer and healthier lives of vegetarians and vegans.

Although breakfast traditions vary vastly from country to country, the underlying principles of good nutrition are the same.

Unrefined starches – breads and cereals, made from whole grains – are basic, along with small amounts of more concentrated foods like seeds and nuts and, VERY IMPORTANT, plenty of fruit or vegetables.

This holds true for the breakfast our Korean guests shared with us: sticky purple rice with cooked vegetables, vegetable soup and dark green crunchy seaweed.

Or the breakfast we enjoyed at a hospital staff canteen in Thailand – rice with a variety of vegetable and bean accompaniments.

Or the breakfast at a seaside café in Vietnam, starting with a heap of pineapple, mango and dragon fruit chunks.

In many countries, the same sort of food is eaten at all the meals.

Spicy Indian breakfasts based on rice and vegetables, Mexican breakfasts with corn and beans, African breakfasts of local starches and vegetables, Chinese breakfasts of rice and greens are all following the same principle.

The important thing is that most of the food should be simple, natural and unrefined.

The recipes here are for a variety of whole unrefined plant-food breakfast dishes that are easy to make and flexible enough to be adapted and used wherever whole unrefined plant foods are available.

Solutions

to some common

breakfast

problems

'Can't face breakfast': cut down on your evening meal and start with a very small breakfast, such as banana or apple, and gradually build up.

'No time to cook in the morning': don't cook; eat fruit, bread and spread. Use packet cereals or cook the night before and reheat.

'Don't like cereals': then eat fruit and a variety of breads and spreads.

'Absolutely no time to eat breakfast': in the long term, change your programme and get up earlier. In the short term, grab some fruit to eat on the way (or you could make a sandwich the night before).

'Can't be bothered fiddling about with recipes': eat bread with a handful of nuts and raisins and go for convenience fruits like apples and bananas.

A guide to
choosing
breakfast menus

Continental breakfast has come to mean a quick, light breakfast, which can be anything from tea and toast to bread with an array of spreads, cereals, orange juice, yogurt and fresh fruit. It varies from country to country.

In France it may just be bread and coffee (croissants on Sundays), but in Germany they add cheese and sliced sausage, and in Hungary there can be tomatoes, cucumber and radishes as well.

Cooked breakfast usually means something savoury to eat with a knife and fork. There are healthy and tasty alternatives to the traditional fry-up with its high content of animal fat and protein.

Another option is the **'everyday healthy plant-food breakfast'**: whole cereal with bread, spread and fruit.

18

Choose **fresh fruit** – have some every day if you can and at least four different kinds each week, choosing seasonal varieties when possible.

Cereals – ring the changes with packet cereals and home-cooked varieties. The different cereal grains each contain their own collection of nutrients and phytochemicals, so choose a variety from day to day.

Cereal toppings – make cereals much more interesting by having a selection of half a dozen things to mix and add – granola, pumpkin seeds, coconut, chopped dates, raisins, chopped or ground nuts, ground flaxseed.

Instead of milk – use soya milk, nut milk, coconut milk, stewed fruit or fruit sauce with dry or cooked cereals.

Breads – vary your whole-wheat with non-wheat crisp-bread, rye bread or oatcakes.

Spreads – try making your own, or buy a couple of whole-nut or seed butters so that you can use two or three varieties in the week. Tapenade is a delicious savoury spread made from olives that the ancient Romans used instead of butter.

Fruit spreads – buy or make your own. Mashed banana makes a very good butter and jam substitute, and avocado is known as nature's butter.

Three **'everyday healthy plant-food breakfast'** menus to help you get started on the better breakfast plan . . .

1) **Fresh fruit** – apples and banana
Cereal – Shredded Wheat
Topping – granola, raisins, and half a sliced banana
'Milk' – soya
Bread – whole-wheat toast
Spread – nut butter and the rest of the banana, mashed

2) **Fresh fruit** – 2-3 apricots, 2-3 strawberries
Cereals – cooked brown rice flakes
Topping – chopped dates and shredded coconut, apple purée
Oatcakes
Spreads – peanut butter, Marmite

3) **Fresh fruit and cereal** – Cool and creamy oatmeal (see p. 46)
Bread – whole-wheat toast
Spreads – tahini and apricot 'jam', tapenade

25

An important nutritional supplement: ground flaxseed

Few people need to buy vitamin or mineral supplements. But it makes sense to supplement your diet with some extra-specially nutritious whole-plant-food items.

Flaxseed is a rich plant food source of the omega-3 fats that are important for the brain and immune system, so it is a valuable addition to breakfast.

Grind some freshly each day in a coffee mill and sprinkle over breakfast cereals. For extra flavour, grind some coriander or caraway seeds with it.

26

Cooked cereals

Breakfast is a good time for eating cereals
– not just packet cereals or porridge, but
everything made from cereal grains.

Whole cereals contain many important
vitamins, minerals, phytochemicals and
fibre, much of which are lost when they are
refined.

For strong nerves, healthy bones, a strong
immune system and good digestion, choose
whole varieties, whether packaged cereals,
hot cooked cereal or bread.

Cook cereals well. Whole grains of wheat need several hours, whole barley at least an hour, brown rice 50 minutes, millet 45-50 minutes.

Rolled or flaked cereals cook much faster, particularly rolled oats, which are already partly cooked.

Meal, for example corn meal, cooks even more quickly.

Do not eat cereals raw, with the possible exception of oats that have been soaked overnight. Well-cooked grains are more nourishing as well as more digestible so, if anything, err on the side of overcooking them.

Quantities: as a rough guide reckon on half a cup of uncooked cereal or a cup of cooked cereal per person.

Oat porridge for two people

1 cup porridge oats to 2½ cups water

• Bring to the boil, stirring occasionally, then turn down heat and simmer for 5 minutes.
• Add more water if you like a thinner porridge.

Some like their porridge plain with soya milk and a little salt, and I have even heard of savoury porridge eaten with a commercial salty relish.

Some suggestions for a delicious bowl of porridge: top with sliced banana, raisins, chopped nuts or granola, ground flaxseed and soya milk and/or soya cream.

Sweet tooth? Drizzle a little honey, maple syrup, apple juice concentrate or black treacle over the top.

Cooking other cereal flakes:

Rice and millet flakes: 1 cup flakes to 2-3 cups water (depending on how thick you want it to be). Make in the same way as oat porridge but cook for about 10 minutes.

Wheat, barley and rye flakes: same proportions, but cook for longer. Barley flakes need at least 20 minutes.

Cracked wheat: cook for 5-10 minutes or simply pour boiling water over it and let it stand for 15 minutes.

Time-saving tip: pour boiling water over cereal flakes and leave for half an hour or longer. This will greatly reduce the time needed to cook them.

Hot cooked cereal variations

Pina colada rice – For one cup of brown rice flakes add 1 cup tinned crushed pineapple and ½ cup shredded coconut and reduce the water by ½ cup.

Armenian barley – To one cup of barley flakes add ½ cup chopped dried apricots, ½ cup raisins and ½ teaspoon (tsp) ground coriander.

Danish rye – To one cup of rye flakes add ½ tsp caraway seeds and 1 tablespoon (tbs) of black molasses.

Special cereal dishes

Here are some delicious breakfast dishes for when you need a change, or maybe for days when there is more time.

You can make most of them partly or completely in advance, and re-heat them in the morning.

Breakfast bread or rice pudding

½ cup cashews
½ cup dates
1½ cups hot water
½ tsp cinnamon
½ tsp vanilla
½ cup chopped walnuts
½ cup raisins
2 cups cooked brown rice, *or* 3 cups
whole-wheat bread cut in ½ inch
(1.5 cm) cubes

• Blend the cashews, dates and water thoroughly, add the cinnamon and vanilla, then pour over the rice or bread cubes mixed with chopped nuts and raisins and bake in a medium deep dish in a moderate oven for 30-40 minutes.
• Serve with sliced banana and 'milk' or creme. Serves 4.

Millet crumble

1½ cups cooked millet
1½ cups orange or pineapple juice
Granola
Bananas

• Blend the first two ingredients until creamy.
(This works best if the mixture is hot – use
freshly cooked millet, or heat the fruit juice.)

• Take a baking dish, 8 inches (20 cm) square or similar size, and put a layer of granola on the bottom.
• Cover this with a layer of sliced bananas. Pour the hot millet mixture over the bananas and top with a thin layer of granola.
• Serve at once or heat in a moderate oven for 10-15 minutes. Serves 4.

Fruit crisp
Topping

¼ cup honey or apple juice concentrate
¼ cup oil
¼ cup water
1 tsp ground coriander
½ tsp vanilla essence
2¾ cups rolled oats
¼ cup whole-wheat flour
½ cup coconut or chopped nuts

Filling

• Use sliced apples or a mixture of fruits, fresh and dried, to fill a large baking dish (8 inches/20 cms square) three quarters full.
• If the fruit is tart, sweeten with chopped dates, apple juice concentrate, pineapple juice or honey.
• With fresh fruit the liquid should come a quarter way up the dish, half way up if dried fruit is added.
• Mix the topping ingredients together and sprinkle over the filling.
• Bake in a moderately hot oven for 45 minutes or until the top is golden brown.
• Serve with nut cream or milk. Serves 6.

Baked oatmeal

1¼ cups porridge oats
½ cup raisins
½ cup chopped nuts
1½ cups apple juice
½ tsp cinnamon
¼ tsp vanilla essence
2 large apples, chopped

• Mix thoroughly, and bake in medium deep casserole dish for 1 hour in a moderately hot oven.
• Serve with nut or soya milk or creme.
Serves 4.

Muesli

Contrary to what most people think, muesli as it's usually eaten here is not a healthy dish.

The original muesli, invented by Dr Bircher Benner more than a hundred years ago, was thoroughly soaked overnight to ensure that the grains were digestible, and the bulk of the dish was the fresh raw fruit that was added in the morning.

Dr Bircher Benner would hardly recognise the indigestible raw flakes and scant dried fruit and nuts called muesli now.

Here is a variation on muesli:

Cool and creamy oatmeal

2 cups porridge oats
2 cups orange juice
½ cup chopped nuts
4-6 cups fresh fruit

• Combine the first three ingredients and refrigerate overnight.
• Just before serving mix in the prepared fresh fruit, such as grated apples, chopped pears, peaches or apricots, berries. Serves 4.

Cooked muesli

Cooked muesli makes a delicious hot cereal. Choose one of the dairy-free muesli mixes with added fruit and nuts.
• Those coarse cereal grains need quite a lot of cooking. The quickest method is to pour boiling water over it and let it soak for ½-1 hour, then cook for 15-30 minutes.
• Use a generous half cup of dry muesli per person and 2-3 times the volume of water, depending on how thick or thin you want it to be.
• Serve with nut or soya milk or creme.

Granola

Granola is delicious, easy to make and keeps well in an airtight box or tin.
• These recipes are very flexible. You can vary the cereal part, using whatever whole cereal flakes you can find (such as millet, rye, wheat) with whatever nuts and seeds you have.
• You can use oil, nut or seed butter, or nuts or seeds ground up with water.
• Sweetening can be honey, malt, fruit juice concentrate or mashed bananas, apple sauce or soft brown sugar.
• The nuts are best slightly chopped, and seeds like sesame or flax are better ground.

• The proportions can be varied, but just be sure to have a crumbly texture, avoiding big lumps because they take longer to cook.
• If you want to include raisins or any other dried fruit, add them after cooking or they will become hard.
• Add a tiny bit of salt if you want to, but it isn't really necessary for most tastes.
• Cook slowly, say at 120°C, checking and stirring occasionally.
• Granola made with oil will brown much more quickly, so needs more careful watching.

Oil-free granola 1

4 cups porridge oats
½ cup coconut
½ cup pumpkin or sunflower seeds
¾ cup chopped nuts, blended with just
enough water to cover them
1 tsp vanilla
3-4 tbs apple juice concentrate

• Mix together thoroughly and spread on two
baking trays.
• Bake in a slow oven until golden brown
and crunchy.
• Check and stir occasionally while baking.

Oil-free granola 2

1-1¼ cups pitted dates, softened in enough
hot water to cover
2 ripe bananas
8 cups rolled oats
1 cup chopped nuts
1 cup coconut
1 cup sunflower seeds
½ tsp vanilla essence

• Blend the first two ingredients until smooth,
then mix thoroughly with everything else.
• Spread about ½ inch thick on trays and
bake in a cool oven for about 1½ hours,
stirring occasionally.

Crunchy granola

2 cups porridge oats
2 cups jumbo oats
½ cup chopped walnuts
½ cup coconut
½ cup pumpkin seeds
¼ cup apple juice concentrate or honey
¼ cup oil
½ tsp vanilla

• Whisk the last three ingredients together
and add to the rest.
• Mix well.
• Spread evenly on a baking tray and bake
in a slow oven, checking every 15 minutes
until it is golden brown and crunchy.

Waffles

Quick and easy waffles for a weekend breakfast treat

Waffles are quick and easy if you have the right equipment, and can easily be made for breakfast.

They can also be made in advance and are very easily reheated in the waffle iron, in a toaster or in the oven or microwave.

This recipe is 100% natural whole food.

Waffles

1 cup sunflower seeds blended smooth in 1 cup water
1 cup porridge oats
1 cup whole-wheat flour
3 cups water

• Blend everything together and cook in a waffle iron until golden brown.
• The batter thickens as it stands, so add more water if it gets too thick to pour easily.
• This recipe makes about eight 6 in/15 cm diameter waffles.

Very light oat waffles

2 cups water or soya milk
2 cups porridge oats
2 tbs sesame seeds
2 tbs flour (whole wheat or any kind)
1-2 tbs oil
1-2 tbs honey (optional)

- Make in the same way as previous recipe.
- Yield: around 6 waffles.

Waffles

Eat waffles with any of the delicious spreads
that you enjoy eating on toast or bread,
including fruit spreads, apple sauce, thick
coconut cream, tahini with honey, maple
sauce, etc.

Or have savoury waffles with humus,
scrambled tofu, fried tomatoes or anything
else that tastes good on bread or toast.

'Milks'
and other things to eat
with cereals

Soya milk is very widely available now, but it is still not always cheap.

If you have a large household who all use soya milk, a soya milk machine is a good investment, as milk can be made for a tenth of what it costs to buy.

(These machines are very useful for making tofu, too.)

It is best not to use the same sort of milk
every day, especially if you are avoiding
dairy milk because of allergies.

You could develop an allergy to soya milk,
so vary the menu, and have a different milk
or a fruit sauce from time to time.

Coconut is another delicious non-dairy 'milk'.

Cashew 'milk' or cream

• Blend 1 cup cashews in 1 cup water until very smooth – about 1 minute, less if you cook them for a few minutes first.
• Add 3-4 cups of water and blend again, briefly, for milk. Add proportionately less for cream.
• You can use other nuts, such as Brazil nuts or almonds, but cashews are the creamiest.

Cashew rice or oat 'milk'

½ cup cashews
½ cup cooked brown rice or cooked oats
(leftover porridge)

• Add enough water to cover and blend
until smooth, then add water as in previous
recipe.
• Stir before serving.

Sesame 'milk'

- Blend light tahini together with 4 or 5 parts of water.
- Add more water as desired.

This is rather an acquired taste, but those who do acquire the taste love it. It's a rich source of calcium.

Sweetening 'milk'

Those who want to can sweeten their milk
with a little apple juice concentrate, honey or
malt, or blend in a couple of softened dates.

A little vanilla or almond essence can be
added too.

Fruit whip

• Blend together 1 cup pineapple or orange juice with a banana and use as milk with breakfast cereal.

Apple sauce

• The quickest way is to wash and roughly chop any sort of apples.
• Cook them with a little water until soft. Transfer to blender and whizz briefly.
• Sieve for a smooth and wholesome apple sauce.
• No blender? Cut the pieces a little smaller and cook for a little longer before sieving.

Breads

As with all the other breakfast foods, variety is good.

Don't only eat whole *wheat* bread, but vary it sometimes with rye bread, mixed grain bread, rye and other crisp-breads, oatcakes or rice cakes.

Spreads

There are all kinds of interesting whole-food alternatives to butter, margarine and jam.

'Butters' and spreads

'Butters'

Butter is high in saturated fat and cholesterol, and margarine is a refined and processed product that often contains milk solids and sometimes unhealthy fats.

Even when you read the labels carefully and avoid hydrogenated oils, trans fats and milk solids, you still have an unnatural product, not ideal for an unrefined plant-food diet.

So what can take their place? Nuts and seeds are naturally high in very healthy oils and make very good whole-food butters.

Peanut butter is available everywhere, but read the labels and choose the whole nut ones without added sugar, oil and salt.

Health food shops usually have a variety of nut butters but they tend to be expensive.

Tahini is sesame purée and can be found in health food shops, some supermarkets, and in Asian food shops.

'Butters' and spreads

Nut butters

• Make small quantities in a coffee grinder or blender.
• Use either raw or roasted nuts. Cashews, peanuts, almonds and hazelnuts make particularly good butters if they are roasted first. (Put them on a tray in a hot oven or under the grill, and watch them carefully as they burn easily.)
• Walnuts, pecans and Brazil nuts make good butters just as they are.

• To make a small amount of nut butter, grind ¼ cup nuts to a fine powder in a coffee grinder.
• You may need to add some water or oil to make it spreadable.
• Add just enough to give it the right consistency.
• Adding water gives an excellent creamy spread that keeps for a few days in the fridge.
• If you use oil rather than water, it will keep for much longer.
• To make nut butter in a blender, grind up one cupful of nuts at a time and add water or oil as needed.

Seed butters

Tahini is sesame seed purée. It keeps very well and as it is very concentrated it goes a long way.

Some people love this thick grey paste straight away. Others need time to acquire the taste, but it's well worth doing so, as tahini is rich in calcium and healthy fats.

Some find it easier to spread if it is creamed by *slowly* stirring in an equal volume of water. (Just cream a small amount at a time, as it doesn't keep for long once water is added.)

You could easily make your own tahini with toasted sesame seeds in the coffee grinder in the same way as nut butters.

You can make sunflower and pumpkin seed butters in the same way.

Two of the healthiest and most delicious butters

Avocado butter

Ripe avocado is a delicious replacement for butter or cream cheese. Simply spread it generously onto your bread.

It goes well with savoury spreads like yeast extract, and is very good topped with sliced tomato or onion.

To make a spread for several people to share, mash a ripe avocado with a little chopped onion, some crushed garlic or garlic purée and salt to taste.

Avocado is also very good with sweet spreads, especially dark fruit spreads.

Banana butter

Just spread fresh ripe banana generously on your bread.

This is very good with nut butter or tahini, and with all kinds of fruit spreads and fresh fruit like berries, grapes or pear, peach or apricot slices.

There are more ideas in the Raw fruit on bread section (see p. 81).

Avocado banana butter

• Mash equal quantities of each together.
• Spread thickly on bread and eat right away. It doesn't keep.

Dried fruit jams

• You can use one or more kinds of dried fruit. For soft, 'ready to eat' dried fruit, you can just pour boiling water over it and let it soak until it's soft, then mash or blend.
• For more chewy dried fruit, you may like to cook it as well.
• Soak first, for an hour or more, then cook gently until it's fairly soft, then mash or blend, or eat it on bread, just as it is.

Date spread

1 cup chopped dates with enough hot water
to cover

• Just soak until soft and stir.

Variations: use orange juice instead of
water; stir in ¼ tsp ground aniseed.

Orange fig spread

• Cook dried figs with enough orange juice to cover them, then blend (add more juice if necessary, but just enough to let the blender blades turn).

Apricot pear spread

• Cook a mixture of dried apricots and dried pears in enough water to cover them.
• Mash or blend, depending on how smooth you like it to be.

Raw fruit on bread

Bananas are perfect for spreading just
as they come, so is ripe sharon fruit
(persimmon) which has the consistency of
jam.

Other fresh fruits like peaches, pears and
apricots can be cut up and arranged on
mashed banana or on nut-buttered bread.

Fruit spreads

Here's a summer breakfast fit for a king – or a foodie:

• Spread bread with nut butter, then with pear and raspberry purée fruit spread, cover with mashed banana and top with fresh raspberries or halved grapes. It's delicious!

Fresh or frozen fruit jams

• Use any sort of fresh or frozen fruit you like.
• Cook briefly and use chopped dates or raisins to sweeten and thicken: 1 cup dates to 1-2 cups fruit, depending on how sweet the fruit is.

Blackcurrant spread

1 cup fresh blackcurrants (use slightly more
if using frozen fruit)
1 cup chopped dates
Water – just enough to cover the dates

• Cook the dates in the water for a few
minutes, then add the fresh or frozen fruit,
bring it to the boil, stir well, then leave it to
cool.
• It will thicken as it cools.
• Add more water for a thinner spread.

Blackberry and cranberry spread

• Use a mixture of cranberries and blackberries instead of blackcurrants.

Cranberry special

1 cup frozen cranberries (use slightly less for fresh cranberries)
¼ cup apple juice concentrate or honey
¼ cup raisins
¼ cup water

• Cook together until the cranberries have popped.

Savoury hot breakfasts

How about a totally vegetarian hot savoury breakfast at the weekend?

These recipes are good to eat on toast. You can add mushrooms (sauté lightly in a little olive oil, and sprinkle with dried tarragon), vegetarian sausages, and perhaps some potatoes.

How about greens at breakfast? Bubble and squeak is easy, too.

Scrambled tofu

1 large onion, chopped
1 stick celery, chopped
2 tbs olive oil with 1 tbs water
1 250g block tofu
1 clove garlic, crushed
1 tbs yeast flakes
1 tsp herb salt
¼ tsp turmeric

• Sauté the first three ingredients together until soft and transparent, then mash or blend before adding the crumbled tofu and seasonings.
• Mix well and heat through.

Easy beans

• Sauté a chopped onion, chopped celery stick and crushed garlic clove in olive oil until soft.
• Add several cups of tinned or pre-cooked beans, a tin of chopped tomatoes, 2 tbs tomato purée, seasonings such as paprika, cumin, fresh coriander.
• Cook gently through and serve with fresh or grilled tomatoes or mushrooms.

Tomatoes Provençal

• Gently sauté a medium-sized onion, chopped or sliced, with a crushed clove of garlic.
• Add several thickly sliced fresh tomatoes or a tin of whole tomatoes, sprinkle with fresh or dried basil, cook gently through, season to taste and serve on toast or with scrambled tofu.

Bubble and squeak

This traditional British dish is simply leftover mashed potatoes and cooked cabbage fried together.

Exact proportions are not important. The healthiest way to do this is to use minimal olive oil in a non-stick frying pan, or to simply mix it all up, put it in a shallow oven-proof dish and brown it in the oven.

Chopped onion and crushed garlic add phytochemicals and give an extra tang.

'Cheeze'

Dairy cheese is a versatile and convenient food that has long been a part of the traditional Western diet.

Now we are learning more and more of the dangers of dairy produce, cheese begins to look less attractive.

All dairy produce is naturally rich in reproductive and growth hormones, and the more mature the cheese, the more oxidised and dangerous the cholesterol.

'Cheeze' recipes

Leaving out cheese can leave a big gap in a vegetarian cook's repertoire so here are some completely plant-food alternatives.

They can be used as spreads, sauces, toppings, and can even be made into sliceable blocks.

These 'vege-cheezes' have several advantages.

First, they lack the high saturated fat and cholesterol levels of dairy produce, with their worrying connections with specific serious diseases.

They also lack the irritant substances that cause food sensitivities such as migraine, indigestion and irritable bowel syndrome in susceptible people.

Third, and most importantly, they contain the health-promoting phytochemicals that occur naturally in their plant food ingredients.

Country Life cashew pimento 'cheeze'

Blend until smooth:
1 cup water
¾ cup cashew nuts or sunflower seeds
2 tbs sesame seeds or tahini
⅔ cup rolled oats
3 tbs yeast flakes
1 small onion
1 level tsp herb salt
1 clove garlic
2 tbs lemon juice, or to taste
½ cup tinned or fresh pimentos (sweet peppers)
⅛ teasp dill seed (optional)

This can be used as it is in lasagne, for pizza topping, or 'cheeze' on toast. To make a spread, cook it until it thickens, stirring all the time.

• For 'cheeze' on toast, spread generously and grill.

• To make into a brick for slicing, mix 4 tbs agar flakes in 1½ cups water and boil until flakes are dissolved.

• Use the above recipe, but substitute the 1½ cups agar mixture for the 1 cup water.

• Blend until creamy then pour into a mould and chill.

Quick 'cheeze' sauce

1 cup cashew pieces cooked for a few
minutes in 1 cup water
3 tbs yeast flakes
1 tsp salt
¼ cup fresh onion
1 clove garlic
½ cup pimento (leave out if you would like a
white 'cheeze')
2 tbs lemon juice

- Blend until very creamy.
- For 'cheeze' on toast, spread it thickly on toast and grill until lightly browned.
- See p. 100 for Pita pizza.
- For a 'cheeze' spread that will keep for several days, cook, stirring constantly, until it thickens.

Pita pizza

This is a very quick and easy kind of pizza, which can quite easily be made for breakfast.

• Carefully split each piece of whole-wheat pita bread into its two layers and spread each layer with pizza toppings.
• Start with a thin layer of tomato sauce if you have it, if not, use tomato or sun-dried tomato paste.

- The 'cheeze' can come next and on top of this can go all sorts of sliced things – onions, peppers, tomatoes, mushrooms, artichoke hearts, vegetarian sausage, or the 'cheeze' can come last, spread or drizzled in a pattern over the top.
- A few olives, and a sprinkle of oregano or other herbs completes it.
- Cook in a hot oven for 10-15 minutes and serve at once.

Savoury continental breakfast

Peanut butter or tahini with Marmite must be the easiest savoury breakfast spread.

There are various vegetarian slicing sausages, pâtés and spreads to buy.

Here are a few more to make at home. Serve them with bread, crisp-bread or toast, along with sliced tomatoes, cucumber, radishes or whatever else you fancy.

Bean spreads

You can give the blender a rest and simply mash the beans.

There are endless variations to be made, so just use your imagination and whatever you can find in your cupboard.

Here are two to start you off. Cook your own beans or open a tin.

Mediterranean: add olive oil, tomato purée, herbs – basil and/or oregano, chopped olives.

English special: mash the beans with a generous amount of Marmite. Mix well, eat on toast.

Humus

1 tin chickpeas (1½ cups)
1 cup tahini
1 small onion
1 clove garlic
3-5 tbs lemon juice

• Blend, adding just enough water to allow
blades to turn.
• Add salt to taste, and 2-3 tbs olive oil if
desired.
• Optional extras – add some chopped fresh
red pepper, sweet paprika powder or fresh
herbs to the mixture in the blender.

Tapenade

Black or green pitted olives and olive oil are
the basic ingredients.
Optional extras to add to 1 tin (1½ cups)
black or green pitted olives (drained)

1-2 garlic cloves (or equivalent garlic purée)
2 tbs chopped onion
2-3 sun dried tomatoes or 1 tbs tomato
purée

• Make it in a food processor or blender, or chop it finely by hand.
• It can be oil free if you have a food processor, but a little oil makes it easier to hold together.
• If you use a blender, add just enough oil to allow the blades to turn easily.

Tofu cottage 'cheeze'

1 250g pack of tofu, mashed
1 tsp garlic purée
1 tsp tarragon or other dried herbs
Salt or herb salt to taste
Lemon juice to taste
Soya milk, creme or mayonnaise

• Mix together, adding enough nut or soya milk, creme or mayonnaise to make it hold together.

Avocado spread

• Mash a ripe avocado with salt and a little fresh garlic or garlic purée.
• Sprinkle with lemon juice to keep it from going brown.
• Option: add finely diced tomato. Spread thickly and eat at once.

Weight problems?

Obesity *is* reversible, if one has the courage and determination *permanently* to change the lifestyle that has caused it.

Obesity doesn't develop in a few weeks, nor can it be overcome in a short time.

Weight problems?

Trying to lose large amounts of weight rapidly is counterproductive: a very spare diet causes the body to go into starvation mode and *conserve* fat, and if one does manage to lose much on such a diet, the starvation mode will ensure that the fat is put on again as soon as the strict regime lets up.

The key is a *permanent* change to a lifestyle that includes vigorous physical activity and a satisfying diet based on unrefined plant foods.

Add sunlight, fresh air, avoidance of alcohol and other harmful substances, plenty of water to drink, and **a cheerful, thankful heart,** and you really can't go wrong.

Not only does the weight problem come under control, but one begins to feel stronger and fitter from the very start.

In fact, losing weight the healthy way puts you in a win-win situation.

114

Food eaten for breakfast is mainly burnt up to provide energy for the day.

Food eaten in the evening, especially near bedtime, tends to be stored up as fat.

The solution is to have a big breakfast, a good lunch and a small light evening meal or, as the old saying goes:

Weight problems?

Breakfast like a king.
Lunch like a prince.
Sup like a pauper!

A total
lifestyle plan
for better
health

NEW START is a rehabilitation programme developed by doctors in the late 1970s at Weimar Institute in California.

It has been particularly successful in helping people with high blood pressure, high blood cholesterol, coronary heart disease, diabetes and weight problems.

NEW START is an acronym for the eight natural remedies:

N for *Nutrition* – simple, natural, unrefined plant foods.

E for regular *Exercise* – brisk walking is excellent.

W for *Water* – remember to drink regularly.

S for *Sunlight* – be sensible and moderate.

T for *Temperance* – abstain from all poisons.

A for *Air* – spend time outdoors daily.

R for regular *Rest* and regular recreation.

T for *Thankfulness* and *Trust in divine power.*

120

Putting the NEWSTART programme into practice:

1) 'Revolutionary' eating plan: 'Breakfast like a king; lunch like a prince; sup like a pauper.'

2) **Totally nutritious plant food:** unrefined plant food with all its nutrients intact and no cholesterol, little saturated fat, lots of fibre and phytochemicals.

Raw food emphasis: something raw at every meal.

Variety: a wide variety of foods from day to day.

Exercise: regular daily exercise, up to one hour or more according to tolerance – preferably in the fresh air and sunlight.

Water: start with a big drink of water when you wake up and drink throughout the day.

Sunlight: we need it to reduce stress, lower cholesterol and produce vitamin D. A light tan protects the skin from sun damage. Use common sense and moderation.

Temperance: moderation in all good things, abstinence form harmful things like caffeine, alcohol, etc.

Air: well ventilated rooms and time outdoors in the most natural environment available.

Rest: adequate sleep at night, weekly rest days and regular holidays.

Trust in divine power: it helps us to develop **thankfulness,** and optimism: the most important of all the healing factors.

126

The blessing of asking a blessing

Feelings of thankfulness actually change the chemistry of the brain.

Endorphins – natural antidepressants and tranquillisers – are released which make you feel good and stimulate all your body systems to work more efficiently.

So do begin your breakfast with a moment of thanksgiving.

You will enjoy it more and it will do you more good.

God is great, God is good,
Let us thank him for our food.
By his hands we are led,
Let us thank him for our bread.